Best of Mozart

For Piano Solo

Arranged by John W. Schaum
Edited by Wesley Schaum

Foreword

The primary object of this album is to serve as an introduction to the music of Mozart. These arrangements enable a student of modest proficiency to gain an acquaintance with many master themes. Familiar music has been selected for maximum student appeal.

The choice of muisc in the collection is determined by its effectiveness for teaching purposes – based on over fifty years experience with thousands of piano students at the Schaum Music School in Wisconsin.

Additional books in this series are:

Best of Bach
Best of Beethoven
Best of Chopin
Best of Strauss
Best of Tchaikowsky

Schaum Publications, Inc.
10235 N. Port Washington Rd. • Mequon, WI 53092
www.schaumpiano.net

Mozart
Biographical Sketch

On the 27th of January, 1756, at Salzburg in the Austrian Tyrol, a child was born who was destined to become one of the greatest composers and who was the most precious musical genius the world has ever known – Wolfgang Amadeus Mozart. In his fourth year he manifested such eager and intelligent interest in his older sister's clavichord lessons, that his father began teaching him as well. Wolfgang also composed little pieces.

His progress was so rapid that in January, 1762, the father ventured to introduce his children to the public on a concert trip to Munich. It was a success, so in September they went to Vienna where the Emperor, Francis I, invited the children to the palace to perform. Mozart traveled far and wide for many years. Audiences were always gracious and complimentary but the financial rewards were meager.

In 1782 he married Constance Weber. Unfortunately a period of real poverty set in. Both he and his wife were emotionally very immature. She was a careless housekeeper and he was an inadequate manager. The monetary returns from his compositions and concerts were unwisely spent and he was never financially secure.

Yet Mozart became one of the brightest stars in the musical firmament. In his music breathes the warmhearted, laughter-loving artist whose genial nature all the slings and arrows of outrageous fortune might wound, but could not embitter. Joy is the keynote of his compositions; the rare note of tragedy or mourning is but a brief minor episode.

Mozart's productivity was astounding and embraced all departments of musical composition including symphonies, operas, concertos, sonatas, piano music, religious masses, chamber music and songs. Ludwig von Koechel (KETCH-el) devoted his whole life to cataloging Mozart's compositions. In his system the code number K492 refers to Mozart's 492nd composition as listed in Koechel's catalogue. In Mozart's short life span of 35 years, he produced so vast a quantity of music that Koechel, who lived to 77 did not quite complete the task.

INDEX

Air in C

(From "Marriage of Figaro" K492)

Moderato ♩ = 108-116

4

Minuet

(Symphony No. 39, K543)

Allegretto ♩ = 116-126

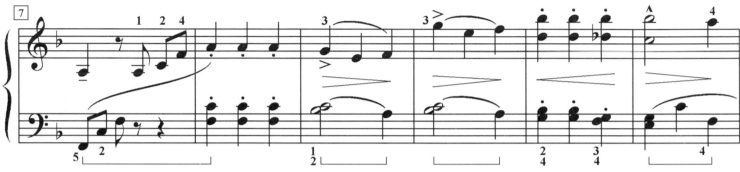

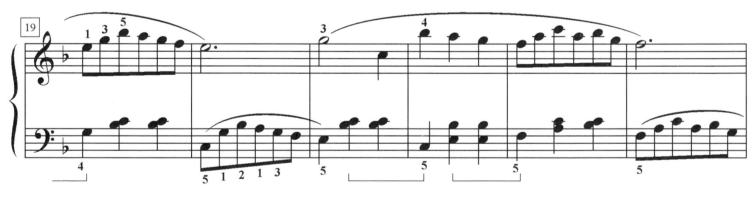

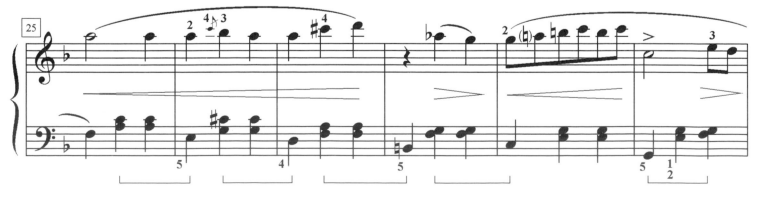

5

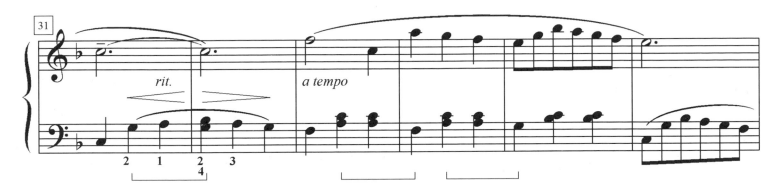

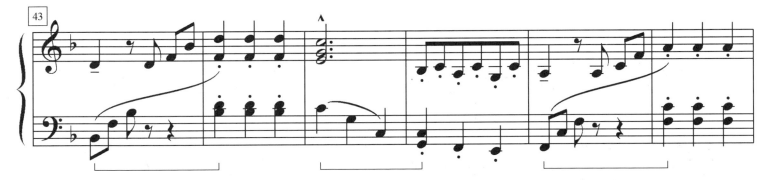

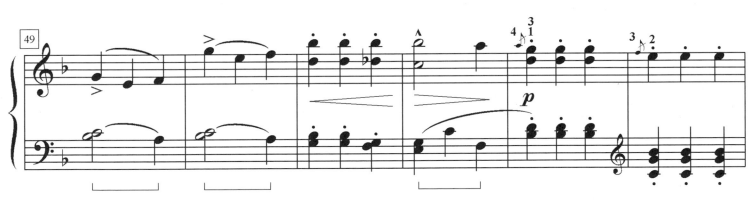

Minuet in G

(K1)

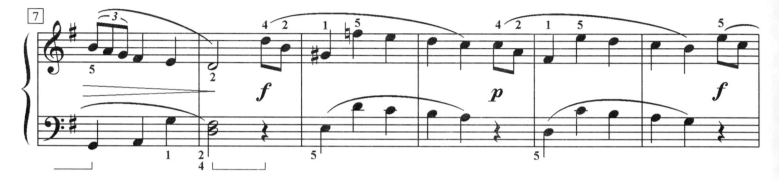

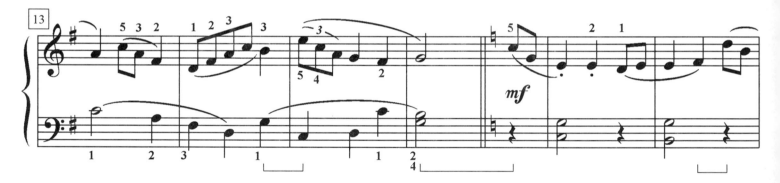

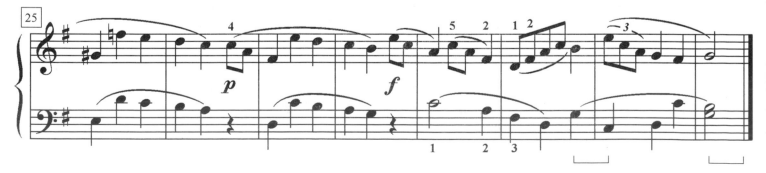

Minuet in F

(K2)

Animato ♩ = 120-132

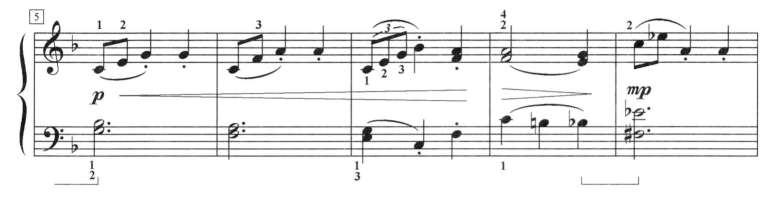

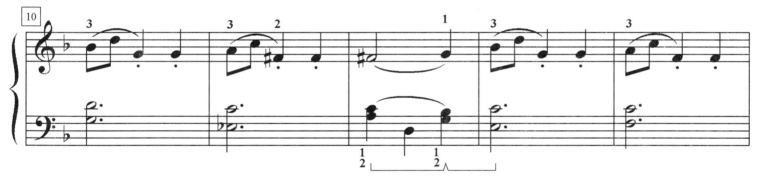

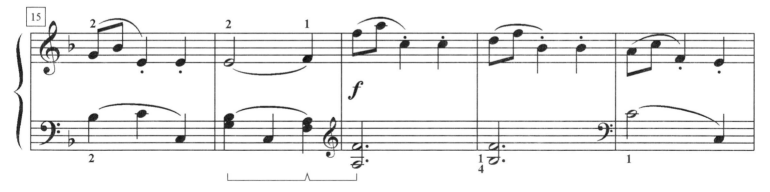

* Play with the 2nd finger; then, while holding the note, change to the 1st finger.

Turkish March

(Sonata in A, K331)

Allegretto ♩ = 100-104

poco   a   poco   cres - cen - do

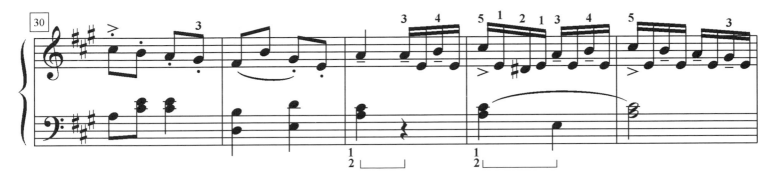

Lullaby*

* Authorities differ on whether Mozart actually wrote this lullaby. However, it has been associated with Mozart for so many years that it is now generally accepted as coming from his pen.

Allegro in B♭

(K3)

Vivo ♩ = 104-112

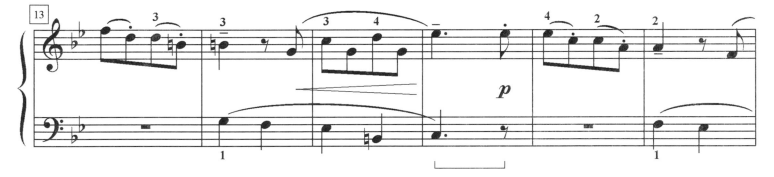

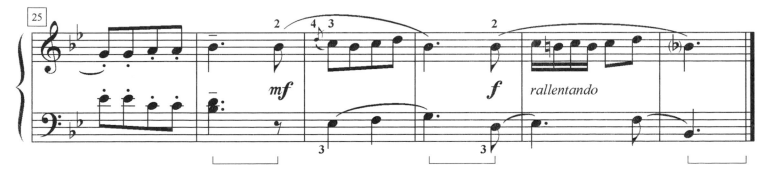

Country Dances

(K606)

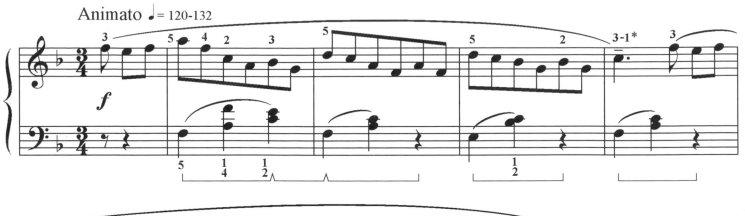

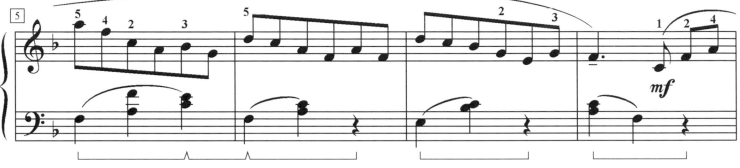

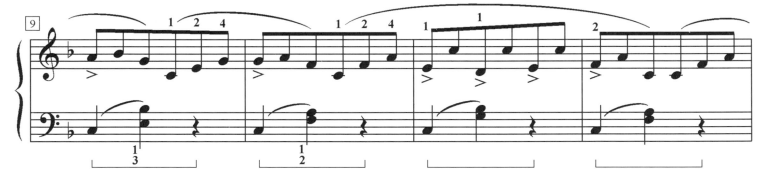

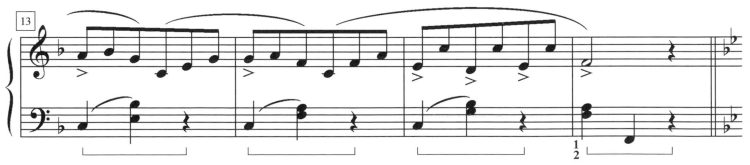

* Play with the 3rd finger; then, while holding the note, change to the 1st finger.

Hand in Hand

(From "Don Giovanni" K527)

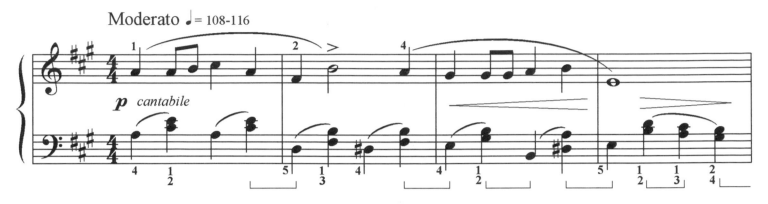

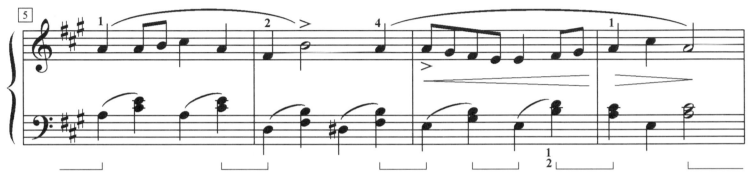

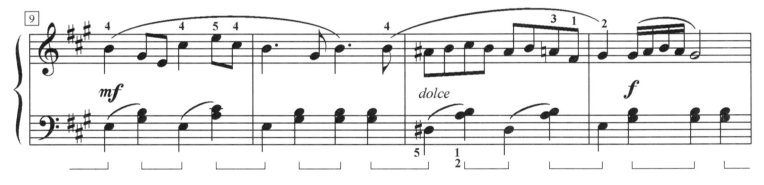

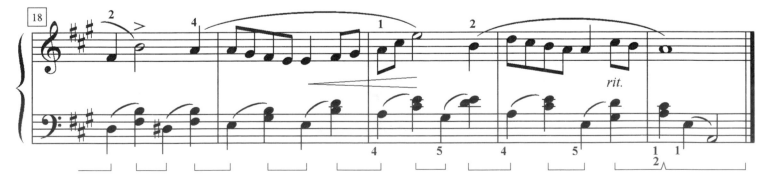

Minuet

(From "Don Giovanni" K527)

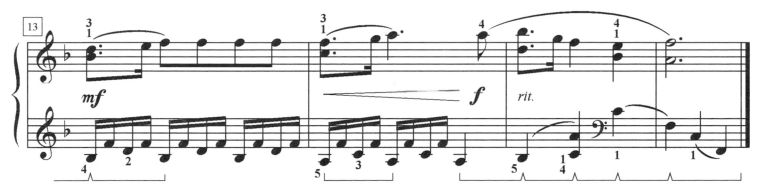

Overture

(From "Marriage of Figaro" K492)

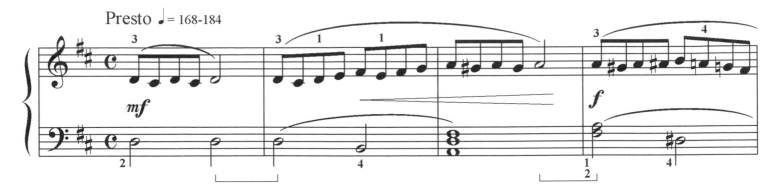

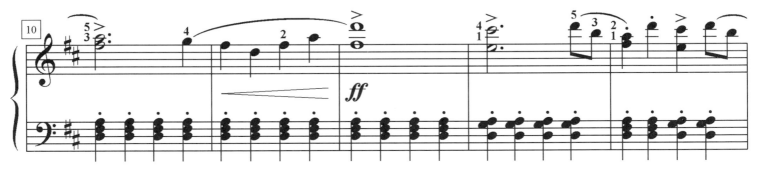

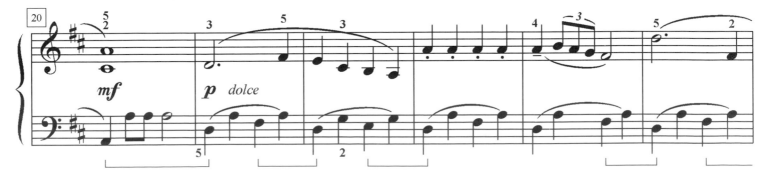

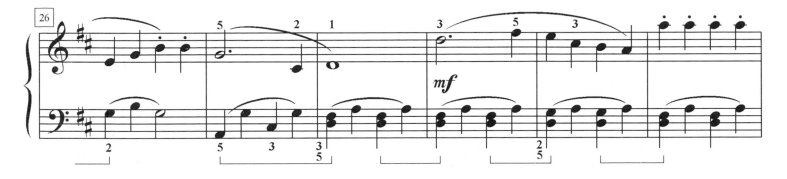

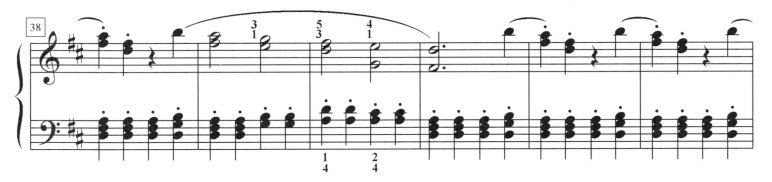

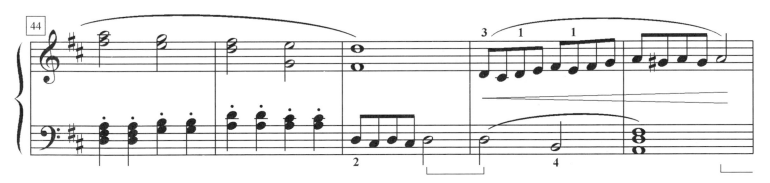

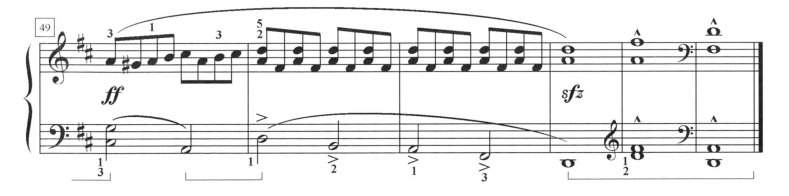

A Little Night Music

(Serenade, K525)

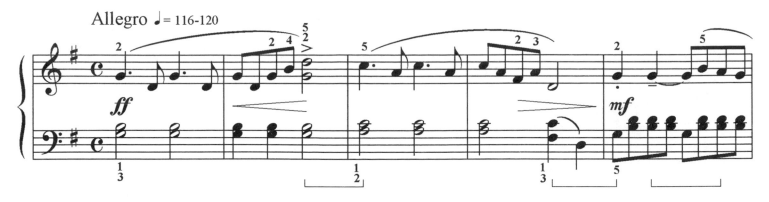

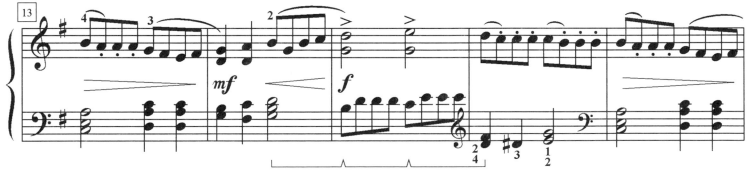

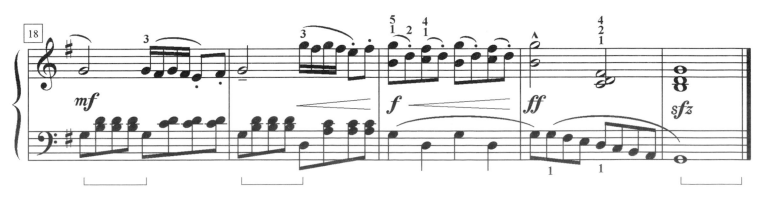

Enchantment

(From "Magic Flute" K620)

Scherzando ♩ = 120-132

Sonata in A

(First Movement, K331)

Andante grazioso ♪ = 120-126

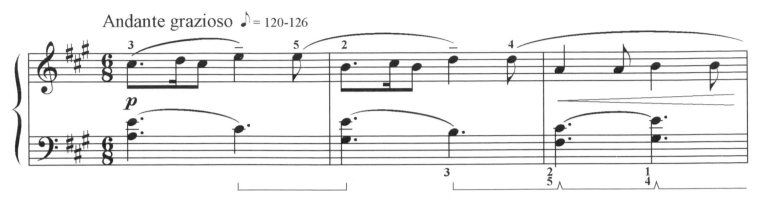

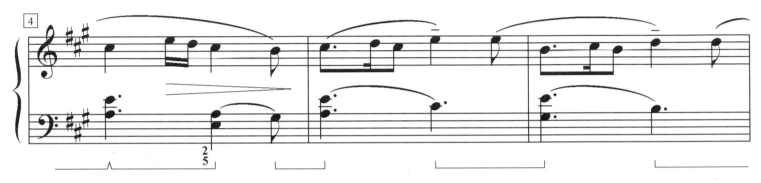

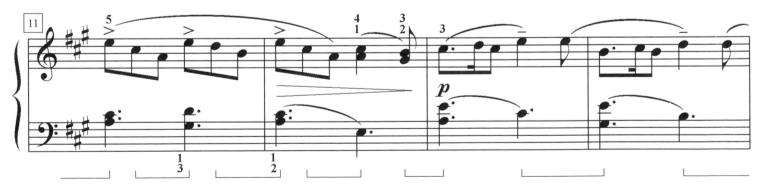

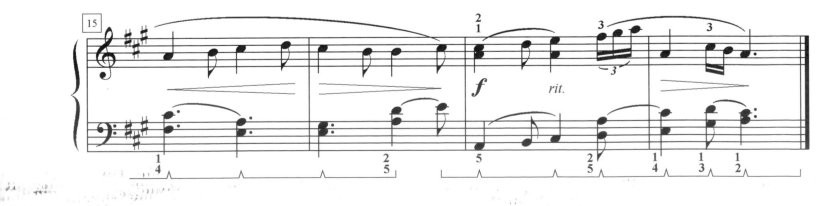

Divertimento

(K334)

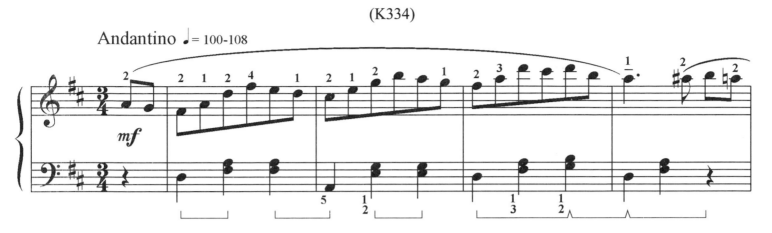

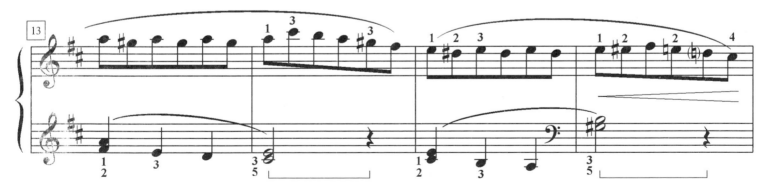

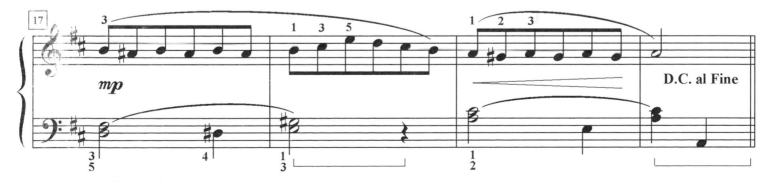

Sonata in C

(First Movement, K545)

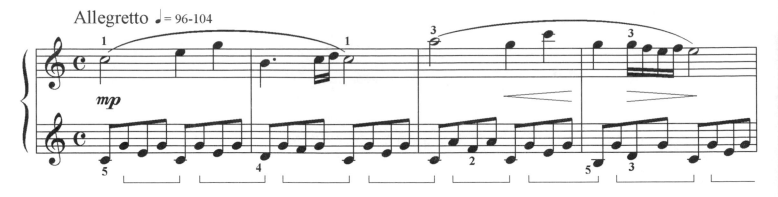

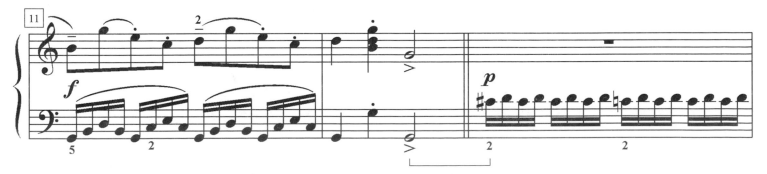

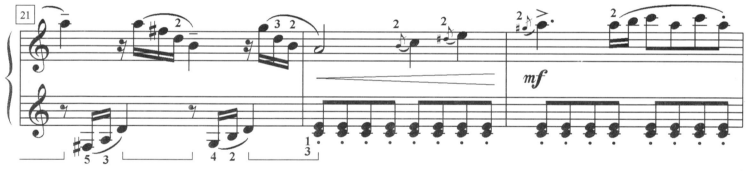

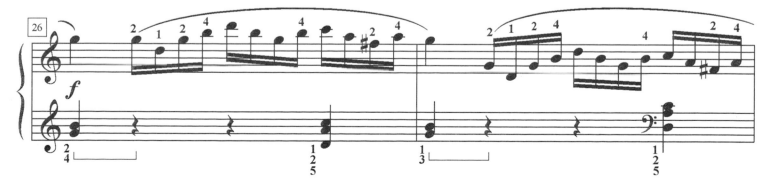

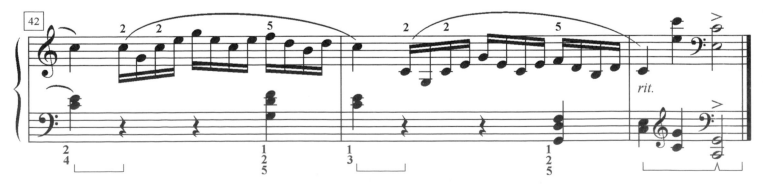